YOUR KING COMES!

A Palm Sunday Celebration

BY JANICE BENNETT WYATT

C.S.S Publishing Co., Inc.
Lima, Ohio

YOUR KING COMES!

Scripture quotations are from the New Revised Standard Version of the Bible, copyright 1989 by the Division of Christian Education of the National Council of the Churches of Christ in the USA. Used by permission.

This service is a revision of "Come, Let Us Welcome Jesus," copyrighted 1980 by C.S.S. Publishing Co.

ISBN: 978-1-55673-406-9   PRINTED IN U.S.A.

**Lo, your king comes to you;
triumphant and victorious is he,
humble and riding on a donkey,
on a colt, the foal of a donkey.**
                — **Zechariah 9:9b**

Production Notes

    This dramatic celebration of the triumphal entry of Jesus into Jerusalem is a "we-were-there" type of re-enactment designed to give all the feeling and experience of being a part of the crowd on that day. It relies on the speaking voice and a minimum amount of action to create the feeling of participation. It is designed to be the sermon portion of your Palm Sunday morning worship service, the day some say is the Children's Day of Holy Week, as a procession or parade is something they can understand. It calls for the participation of children, youth and adults and could be adapted for use in churches of many different sizes. Costumes and action could be added to make it more dramatic, however this also calls for more preparation time.

    As printed here the production could be presented without requiring extra rehearsal time outside of that already planned for church and church school. The first step would be a meeting of the teachers for a full reading of the script. They then could choose children and youth to which the parts would be assigned. Teachers could enlist the participation of those in their own classes, hand out marked scripts and ask those chosen to memorize the part underlined as well as to read and become familiar with the entire script. A reading of the script and assignment of locations could take place during church school time on one of the Sundays prior to Palm Sunday. On Palm Sunday itself the final rehearsal could take place during the church school time if it precedes your regular morning worship service.

    It is suggested that the children and youth participating be seated at the ends of the pews, both on the main aisle and at the far ends of the rows. They should be in their places about 20 minutes prior to the beginning of the service and each should have a small bundle of palms. As the congregation is seated they would hand a palm to all who come to sit in their row. Nursery, kindergarten and grade one members might come in

5

closer to the beginning of the service and sit in groups near the front.

Key to the entire production would be planning and rehearsing enough so that the voices can be heard by all. Remind participants that the parts need to be spoken clearly and with a loud voice, such as one would use when calling a message to someone upstairs or way down on a lower level. If the various parts are memorized, the production will be more effective. All participants and teachers need a copy of the script to clue them as to when their part comes.

You might choose to use the service suggested here beginning on page 9, or design your own. The service bulletin should relay the fact that the congregation is asked by the narrator to join in the re-enactment by repeating words of praise as indicated and by standing and raising their palms when requested.

The narrator should be a strong leader — either the pastor or another leader with a well trained voice and a compelling manner. The two interpreters would most likely be chosen from among your youth. These three should schedule a rehearsal in addition to those scheduled for all participants. The 12 disciples could wear large cardboard name tags so all could easily read their names. This would make the experience even more educational. In addition to the above there are about 30 voices, some more childlike than others. If your presenting group is smaller in number, some could take two parts. In order to have even the smallest children's voices heard you will find that nursery, kindergarten and first-grade children are treated as groups. Each group has a sentence which should be spoken in unison. These lines could be practiced several times in their own classrooms.

Participants stand when it is time for their part and remain standing until the end of the hymn which follows the re-enactment. Suggested locations in the sanctuary for participants: Seat the 12 disciples on the main aisle and have them face the center when they stand. Those who speak first should be seated toward the rear and those who speak later in the middle and front pews. This will give the illusion that the procession is moving forward. The couple owning the colt should be near the back and those speaking after that should be placed in the middle and front pews. Those participants who seem to be in conversation with one another should be placed near each other. The Jesus voice should be a strong one with the ability to convey calmness and conviction. This voice should come from the balcony or another strategic location where the person would not be in full view.

Voices Needed

Narrator	Martha
Interpreters 1 and 2	Child 3 and 4
Jesus	James
Bartholomew	Simon
Andrew	Scribe 1 and 2
Owner of Colt	John
Owner's Wife	Thomas
Matthew	James
Philip	Thaddaeus

Family
  Child 1 and 2
  Mother and Father
	Simon Peter

	Kindergarten
Villagers 1-16	Nursery
Pharisee 1 and 2	First Grade
Mary	Loud Adult

Your King Comes!

Order Of Service

Note before we worship: Children and youth seated at the ends of the pews will distribute palms to you as you enter. Adults are requested to assist the children with following the service and guiding them if necessary. We are all part of the family of God; let us help one another! Think on these things: Is our church really acting like a family? A family of God? What can I do to live out my part? To help our church family to be closer to God?

Prelude

Call To Worship

Leader: God is here! Let us rejoice at his presence.

People: **Let us break forth in shouts of praise and in songs of joy!**

Leader: Listen, O God, to our songs and our prayers and respond to the hearts that reach out for you. Amen.

Processional Hymn *(All Glory Laud and Honor)*

Call To Penitence

O God, Our King and Our Lord, like the crowds that surrounded the Christ on that first Palm Sunday, we often praise you with our lips only to reject you in our hearts. Take disloyalty and unfaithfulness out of our lives and hear us now as we pray together asking for your forgiveness . . .

Confession Of Sin *(in Unison)*

Lord Jesus, as we celebrate your triumphal entry into Jerusalem, help me to search within myself to discover where I stand in the crowd. Am I among those who would deny you because you want me to do things in a way that is different? Do I really want you to be my King when you lead me to give and serve rather than take? Forgive me when I do not make the necessary effort to follow your teachings. Amen.

Kyrie *Lord, Have Mercy Upon Us*

Assurance Of Pardon
Now hear this: God loves you whether you are with those who welcome Jesus or among those who deny him. Be assured God is your Loving Father.

Minister: O Lord, open our lips.

People: **And our mouths shall show forth thy praise.**

Gloria Patri

Litany of Greatness* *(Based on Matthew 23:1-12)*
Leader: Greatness is not:

People: **Letting the happiness of life pass us by, nor forgetting the joy of serving the Lord.**

Leader: Greatness is not:

People: **Preaching without practicing, laying heavy burdens on people.**

Leader: Greatness is not:

People: **Doing things to be seen by the crowd, always picking seats of honor at the banquets.**

Leader: Greatness is:

People: **Being a servant of the Great God, who made Heaven and earth, and being responsible for the world he has entrusted to us.**

---

*Litany titled *Greatness Is* by David James Randolph, *ADVENTURES IN WORSHIP,* Abingdon Press, Nashville, Tennessee, p. 60.

Leader: Greatness is:

People: Following the way of Jesus Christ and through the Spirit making ourselves available to those in need.

Leader: Greatness is:

People: Belonging to the church and making our ministry real in private and public life.

Unison: Greatness is bringing the greatness to God to bear on the greatness of the world's needs. O God, help us to be your servants and the servant of others around our world through Jesus Christ, our Lord. Amen.

Choral Anthem

Your King Comes! *(Palm Sunday Celebration)*

Hymn *Rejoice, You Pure in Heart*

Prayers *(Pastoral Prayer and Lord's Prayer)*

Prayer Response

Concerns Of The Church

The Offertory Sentence

Receiving Of Tithes And Offering

The Offertory Anthem

Presentation Of The Offering And Doxology

Prayer of Dedication

Recessional Hymn *All Hail the Power of Jesus' Name*

Benediction *(Congregation will read responsively)*

Leader: Christ be with us.

People: Christ within us.

Leader: Christ beside us.

People: Christ to win us.

Leader: Christ to comfort.

People: And restore us.

Leader: Christ beneath us.

People: Christ above us.

Leader: Christ behind us.

People: Christ before us.

Leader: Amen.

People: Amen.

Benediction Response

Silent Meditations And Chimes

Postlude

Your King Comes!

A Palm Sunday Celebration

A re-enactment of the triumphal entry of Jesus led by the children and youth of the church school. Adults are asked by the narrator to join in the re-enactment by repeating words of praise as indicated, by standing and raising their palms.

Narrator: Jesus was with his disciples traveling toward Jerusalem, as it was the time of the Passover.

Interpreter 1   Jewish people came to Jerusalem from all over the Mediterranean world so that they could celebrate the Feast of the Passover in the holy city. The most important temple, the center of all Judaism was within the city walls.

Interpreter 2:   The Passover celebration helped them to remember that God had led their forebears out of slavery in Egypt to a land of their own. God had watched over them and protected them as they traveled. He had made it possible for them to be free persons, no longer bound to serve a master whose aims were not their aims.

Narrator: They traveled to Jerusalem in caravans. Many came on foot, walking every step of the way; others traveled by riding on a donkey or a camel; some even came by ship.

13

Interpreter 1: Before Passover was to be celebrated the Jews mended all the roads and bridges, painted the family tombs, washed all the household utensils. Each family threw away all the old leaven that was left from their bread-making. They did this to remember the time their forefathers had to leave Egypt quickly without any provisions for their journey.

Interpreter 2: Jews came from throughout the countryside to Jerusalem to purify themselves once more and to partake of the feast with their families.

Narrator: And so it was that Jesus and the disciples traveled together toward Jerusalem, as was the custom. They went even though Jesus knew it might be dangerous for him.

Interpreter 1: The journey was a slow one. Jesus and the disciples stopped along the way to teach, to heal, to see friends, to greet strangers who had questions.

Interpreter 2: See, now they are approaching the city gate; let's pretend we are there. We can hear Jesus say . . .

Jesus: Andrew, Bartholomew, go into the village over there outside the wall, and just as you are entering, you will see a colt hitched to a post. It's a colt on which no one has ever ridden. Loosen him and bring him here.

Bartholomew: But Master, what shall we say to the owners if they ask why we are untethering him?

Jesus: Simply say, the Lord has need of him and they will understand and let you bring him to me. We will return it later.

Narrator: This was done, John explains in his Gospel, because it was written in the Scriptures studied at that time. We now call that book Zechariah in the Old Testament. You will find it in Zechariah, chapter 9, verses 9-11.

Interpreter 1: Rejoice greatly, O daughter Zion! Shout aloud, O daughter Jerusalem! Lo, your king comes to you; triumphant and victorious is he, humble and riding on a donkey, on a colt, the foal of a donkey. He will cut off the chariot Ephraim and the war horse from Jerusalem; and the battle bow shall be cut off, and he shall command peace to the nations; his dominion shall be from sea to sea, and from the River to the ends of the earth.

Narrator: And they that were sent, went their way and came to the place where the colt was tied, and everything was exactly as Jesus had told them. They began to unloosen the tether . . .

Interpreter 2: The owners of the colt were nearby and called out . . .

Owner: Stop! Why are you unloosening my colt?

Andrew: Jesus of Nazareth sent us to get him. He said to tell you the Lord has need of him.

Owner: Jesus of Nazareth? If that is so, take the colt to Jesus. I have heard of the great things he is doing in the name of the Lord. I am glad to help him. Where is Jesus? I would like to meet him.

Bartholomew: Come along. Many seem to be gathering along the roads who also want to catch a glimpse of him.

Andrew: Yes, they have heard that he raised Lazarus from death to life.

Owner's Wife: Look! A great crowd is gathering. Hurry, I want to be a part of it.

Narrator: The chief priest and Pharisees seem to be gathering over there — they don't seem in the mood to celebrate.

Interpreter 1: No, the chief priests, scribes and Pharisees, the leaders of the Jewish religion, the keepers of the law, were against Jesus as his teachings were different from theirs; they could not believe he was truly the son of God.

Andrew: Here's the colt, Jesus. Come sit upon his back so all can see you above the crowd.

Matthew: I'll put my robe on him for you to sit on.

Philip: Here's mine too. The crowds are getting larger. Be careful, Jesus. We must stay together.

16

Child 1: Give me that palm branch there, Father, so I might wave it.

Mother: I have picked these flowers. I'll throw them in front of him so he knows we like what he is doing and saying.

Child 2: I want to see the new King. Will he save us from the Romans?

Father: I wonder. He tells us to love everyone, but how can we love those who plot against us?

Villager 1: There is much of his teaching that seems hard to follow, but wouldn't we have a wonderful world if all could love their neighbors as they love their own families? But it is so hard to do.

Villager 2: There he comes; I see him. Welcome to the Son of the Family of David!

Family & Villagers 1&2: Hosanna! Blessed be he who comes in the name of the Lord!

Pharisee 1: You see, the world has gone after him, the only way to stop him is to arrest him.

Pharisee 2: We must move quickly now. I wonder if we could persuade one of his followers to help us?

Villager 3: I'm going to throw my robe out for him to go over; that will show him and everyone that he is important.

Villager 4: I'll cover this part of the way with branches from the palm tree.

Family:	Hosanna to the son of David!
Villagers 1-4:	Hosanna in the highest — Hosanna! Blessed be he who comes in the name of the Lord.
Villager 5:	He healed the blind man you know.
Villager 6:	He helped me to walk again. I had been crippled for so long.
Mary:	It is so wonderful that he was able to raise our brother Lazarus from the death that had overtaken him.
Martha:	I still can hardly believe it is true. God is truly with Jesus.
Villager 7:	Rejoice! Rejoice! Here comes the prophet Jesus.
Villager 8:	He is from Nazareth of Galilee, you know. I know the family.
Villager 9:	He cured my daughter who was ill for such a long time, we thought she would never be well again.
Child 3:	I like the way he tells us stories. He even plays games with us. It is good to be near him.
James:	Isn't it great to be welcomed to Jerusalem like this? Jesus' teachings have been heard by many — our world will be a better place because of his teachings.
Simon:	Yes, I believe he is God's son. Otherwise, how could he perform such miracles and speak with

real authority? Hundreds want to hear him talk and teach.

Villager 10: I hear he cured a man of leprosy.

Philip: You're right. I was there when he did it . . . and he is not the only one that Jesus has healed. It seems he can heal anyone who really believes he can do it. Jesus is truly close to God.

Scribe 1: Watch carefully now. Stay close so we might hear what the man teaches. He will surely disobey one of the laws, just as when he picked the wheat on the Sabbath Day.

Scribe 2: Don't worry, I'll watch. I know we have to get him. I'll stay as close to him as I can. He is dangerous for these people — they think he really is their Savior. He will get us into trouble with the Romans.

Child 4: He's coming close to us now, Mother. I want to say hello to him. Lift me up so I can see him. I'll wave this palm branch so he sees me.

Villager 10: Blessed be he who comes in the name of the Lord.

Narrator: Let's call it out so he looks our way. Everyone now. Blessed be he who comes in the name of the Lord!

All: Blessed is he who comes in the name of the Lord.

John: Be careful, Master, the crowd is pressing closer to us. There are so many people. I'm glad they recognize you as their leader.

Thomas: But there are some in the crowd who are enemies, don't forget that. We will stay and watch on this side; you three watch along that side.

James: Is everyone here? Where is Judas? He is not with us now. I can't see him.

Thaddaeus: He stopped to talk to someone quite a ways back, he'll catch up.

Simon Peter: I'll go ahead — I'm tall enough to see above the crowd. I see the Temple ahead now. Shall we head toward it, Master?

Villager 11: You know, about a year ago, Jesus looked at me and knew my thoughts. I've had a new life since then. He is truly amazing, he is close to God.

Villager 12: He cured my sickness. I was out of my mind until I met him and he looked at me and healed me. Just like that — *(snap fingers)*.

Villager 13: Let's just stand back here and watch. I don't want to participate. Someone might see us and think we are his followers.

Villager 14: Yes, I believe Jesus is a great leader, but I don't want to get involved. It is too dangerous.

Villager 15: That Jesus doesn't care who he talks to. He is seen with those that do wrong — sinners, and even tax collectors.

Villager 16: I wonder what does he want from us? I wonder why he cares what we do?

Kindergarten: Hooray for Jesus!

Nursery: He loves everyone.

First Grade: Let's clap our hands and shout Hooray!

Narrator: Let's all do as the children say — join in the clapping and shout Hooray. *(begin clapping)*

All: Hooray!

Narrator: Hooray for Jesus!

All: Hooray for Jesus!

Narrator: Hosanna to the Son of David!

All: Hosanna to the Son of David!

Loud Adult: Be our King, Jesus. Save us from our oppressors, from those who treat us like servants, and make us pay high taxes.

Jesus: Listen to me — I want to be king of your heart and your mind. I want to lead you to love God with all your heart, and all your strength and all your mind. I want to teach you to love your neighbor as yourself.

Narrator: Hosanna! Hosanna! Come, let us all stand, raise your palms high and shout Hosanna!

All: Hosanna!

Narrator: Blessed is he who comes in the name of the Lord.

All:	Blessed is he who comes in the name of the Lord!
Narrator:	Blessed is he who comes from on high!
All:	Blessed is he who comes from on high!
Narrator:	Hosanna in the Highest!
All:	Hosanna in the Highest!
Narrator:	Rejoice you pure in heart — come — let's all sing it together.

www.ingramcontent.com/pod-product-compliance
Lightning Source LLC
Chambersburg PA
CBHW071812020426
42331CB00008B/2477